A Note to Parents

DK READERS is a compelling program for beginning
readers, designed in conjunction with leading literacy
experts, including Dr. Linda Gambrell, Director of the
Eugene T. Moore School of Education at Clemson
University. Dr. Gambrell has served on the Board of
Directors of the International Reading Association
and as President of the National Reading Conference.

Be   read stories
photo   series.
to off   child's
Each   ills,
intere
gene

Tl   at
differ   oose
the b

Pre-l
Leve
Leve
Leve
Leve

T
child
from
leve

N
you
your ch

LONDON, NEW YORK, MUNICH,
MELBOURNE, and DELHI

Series Editor Deborah Lock
U.S. Editor Elizabeth Hester
Senior Art Editor Sonia Moore
Production Allison Lenane
DTP Designer Almudena Díaz
Jacket Designer Katy Wall
Photographer Andy Crawford
Consultant Dr. Aviva Schein

Reading Consultant
Linda Gambrell, Ph.D.

First American Edition, 2005
05 06 07 08 09 10 9 8 7 6 5 4 3 2 1
Published in the United States by DK Publishing, Inc.
375 Hudson Street, New York, New York 10014

Published in Great Britain by Dorling Kindersley Limited

Library of Congress Cataloging-in-Publication Data
Lock, Deborah.
   A trip to the doctor / written by Deborah Lock.-- 1st American ed.
   p. cm. -- (Dk readers. Level 1)
   ISBN 0-7566-1137-7 (pb) -- ISBN 0-7566-1136-9 (plc)
   1. Children--Medical examinations--Juvenile literature. 2. Children-
-Preparation for medical care--Juvenile literature. I. Title. II. Dorling
Kindersley readers. 1, Beginning to read
   RJ50.5.L63 2005
   618.92'0075--dc22

                              2005001089

Color reproduction by Colourscan, Singapore
Printed and bound in China by L Rex Printing Co., Ltd.

Photographs taken at Brentfield Medical Centre
with thanks to Dr. Roland Hughes.
Thanks also to all the models: Freddie Feltham, Su Yin Chan,
Gillian Flashman, and Michelle Gibbins.
Many thanks to "Bearwithlove.com" for their loan of the doctor
and get-well teddy bears. Thanks also to P.C.Werth Ltd.
for their loan of the audiology equipment, and to
the Scrub Factory™ for the nurse's uniform.

All other images © Dorling Kindersley Limited
For further information see: www.dkimages.com

Discover more at
www.dk.com

A Trip to the Doctor

Written by Deborah Lock

DK Publishing, Inc.

Jake was brushing his teeth
after breakfast.
"Are you ready?" called Mom.
"Your checkup with
the doctor is today."

"But I feel fine!"
said Jake,
hurrying into the hall.

At the doctor's office,
Jake and Mom went to the
reception [re-SEP-shun] desk.
The receptionist checked Jake's
name on her records.

"Please take a seat
in the waiting room,"
said the receptionist.

receptionist

Jake sat down and read his book.
After a few minutes, a nurse
came and called Jake's name.

"I'll check a few things first
and then your doctor
will see you," said the nurse.

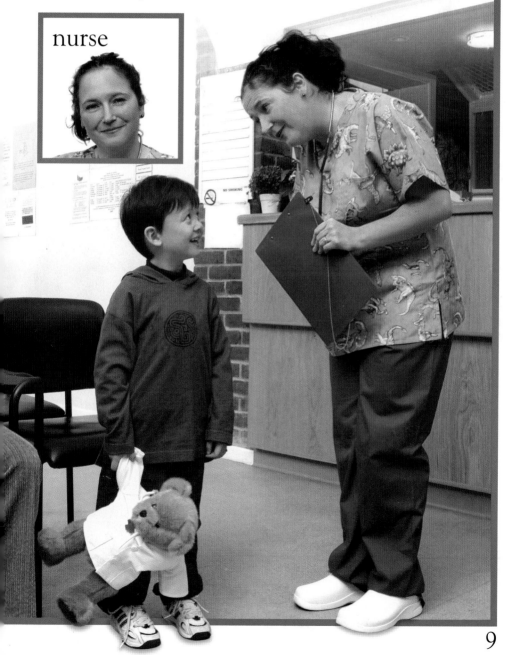

nurse

In the checkup room,
Jake took off his shoes.
He stepped onto the scale.

scale

Then he stood against
the height chart.
The nurse wrote down
the numbers on Jake's medical
[MED-i-cal] records.

The nurse said, "Now I'll check how well your heart is pumping blood through your body."

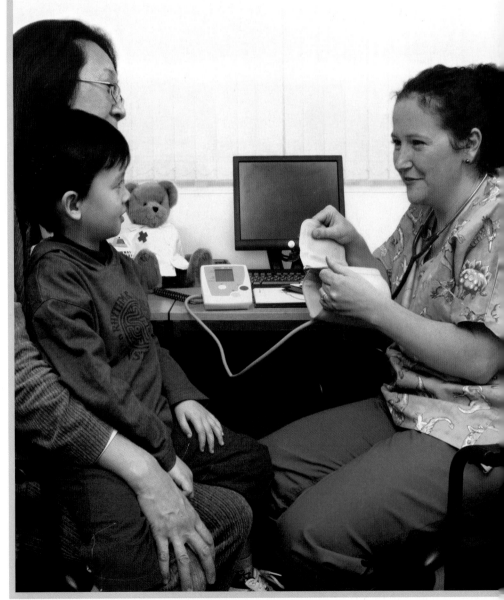

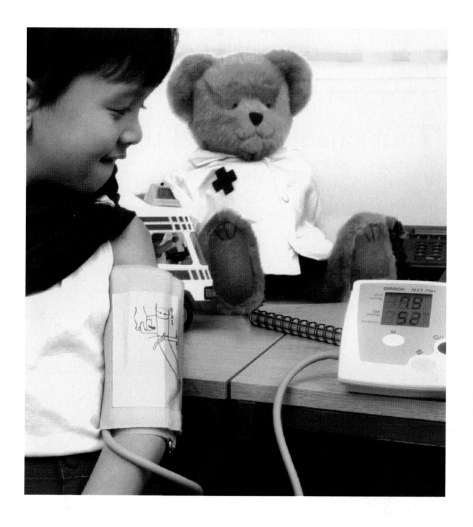

She put a cuff on Jake's arm.
"It's like a small balloon," she said.
It became tighter and tighter
as it filled with air. Nevada Public Library

The nurse watched the numbers on the meter as the cuff began to lose air.

"That's healthy!" said the nurse.

Then she took Jake's temperature [TEM-pur-a-chure] using a thermometer [ther-MOM-i-ter].

thermometer

"Hello, Jake," said Dr. Hill,
as she entered the room.
She looked at Jake's records.

"You look well.
Is your diet
healthy?"
she asked.

doctor

"I eat fruit and vegetables every day," said Jake.

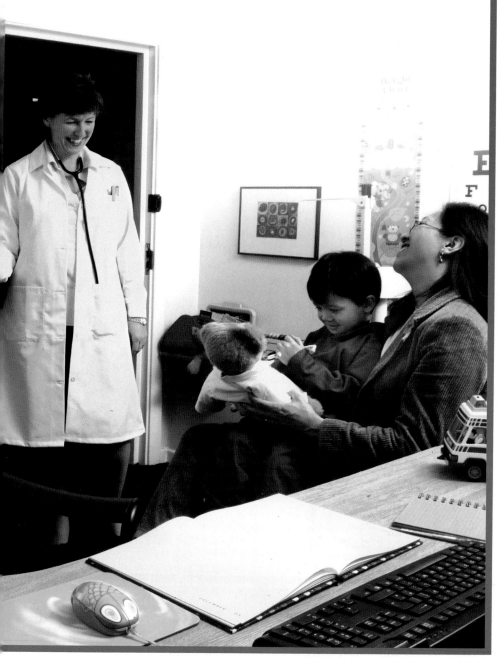

"I'll be checking to see that your body is working just right," said Dr. Hill.

"This is a stethoscope [STETH-a-scope].

It lets me hear your heartbeat and your lungs."

She pressed the round, cool part against Jake's chest and back.

stethoscope

School Bus.

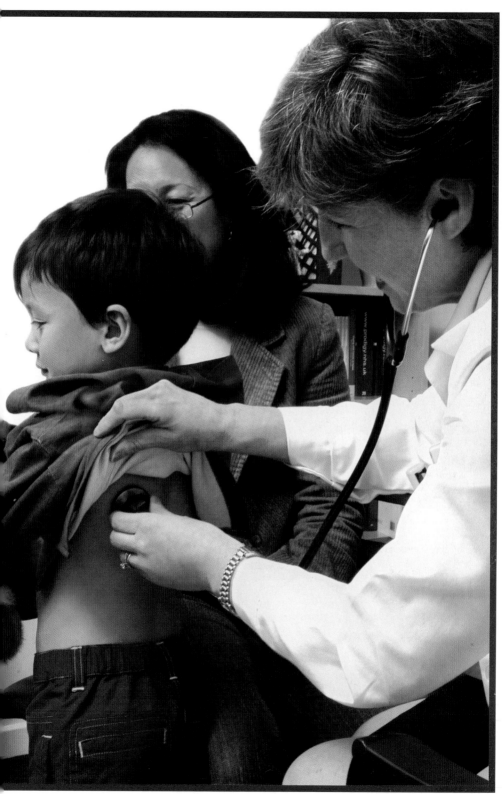

19

Dr. Hill checked Jake's ears,
nose, and mouth.
Jake sat very still.

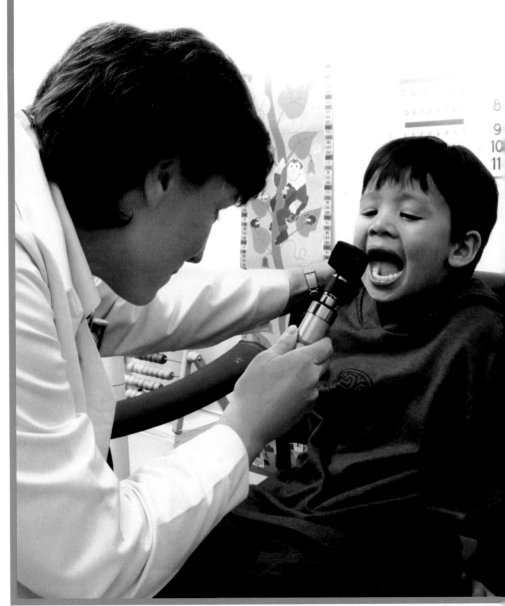

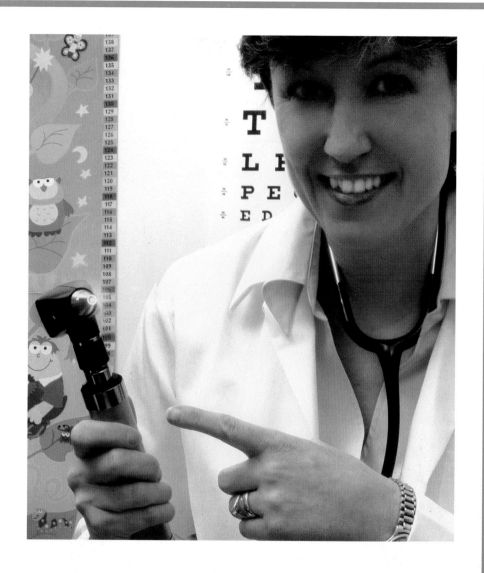

"This light helps me to see
if there are any infections
[in-FEK-shunz]," Dr. Hill said.
"I'm also checking your teeth."

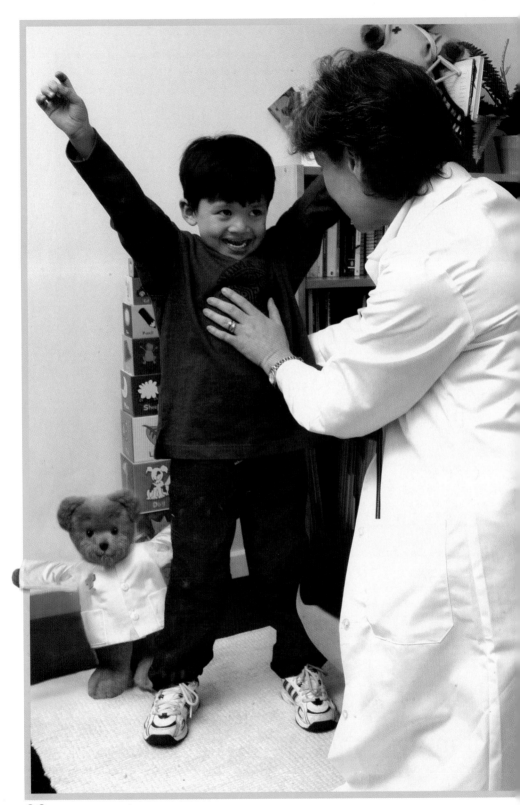

Dr. Hill checked different
parts of Jake's body.
"These all look and feel
healthy," she said.
"Do you exercise every day?"

"I ride my bicycle," said Jake.
"Do you wear a helmet?"
asked Dr. Hill.
Jake nodded.

helmet

"Now I'll check how well you can hear and see," said Dr. Hill.
Jake put on some earphones.

He pointed to the ear
where he heard a sound.

earphones

Jake read some letters on a wall chart.

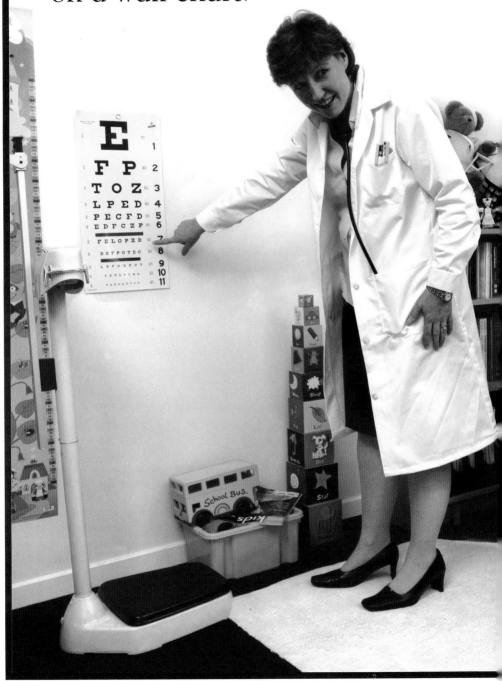

He covered one eye
and then the other.
"Remember, watching television
can strain your eyes," said
Dr. Hill, "so don't watch too
much or sit too close."

"Now, do you have any questions?" asked Dr. Hill. "Is Jake up-to-date with his booster shots?" asked Mom.

Dr. Hill nodded.
Jake talked to Dr. Hill about
how he was doing at school.

Outside the doctor's office,
Jake said to his Mom,

"It was smart to meet Dr. Hill.
Now she'll know all about me
when I am sick."

"Good-bye!"

Picture word list

receptionist

page 7

doctor

page 16

nurse

page 9

stethoscope

page 18

scale

page 10

helmet

page 23

thermometer

page 15

earphones

page 25